The 60-Minute Active Training Series

HOW TO BRING OUT THE BETTER SIDE OF DIFFICULT PEOPLE

PARTICIPANT'S WORKBOOK

Mel Silberman and Freda Hansburg

Pfeiffer

Published by Pfeiffer
An Imprint of Wiley
989 Market Street, San Francisco, CA 94103-1741   www.pfeiffer.com

For additional copies/bulk purchases of this book in the U.S. please contact 800-274-4434.

Pfeiffer books and products are available through most bookstores. To contact Pfeiffer directly call our Customer Care Department within the U.S. at 800-274-4434, outside the U.S. at 317-572-3985 or fax 317-572-4002 or www.pfeiffer.com.

Pfeiffer also publishes its books in a variety of electronic formats. Some content that appears in print may not be available in electronic books.

ISBN: 0-7879-7358-0

Acquiring Editor: Martin Delahoussaye

Senior Production Editor: Dawn Kilgore

Director of Development: Kathleen Dolan Davies

Manufacturing Supervisor: Becky Morgan

Developmental Editor: Susan Rachmeler

Interior Design: Erin Zeltner

Editor: Rebecca Taff

Printed in the United States of America

Printing 10   9   8   7   6   5   4   3

CONTENTS

ABOUT THIS BRIEF TRAINING SESSION

Unfortunately, we can't give "makeovers" that will turn difficult people into delights. But if we put some energy into getting curious, rather than furious, with people we find challenging, often we can gain perspective and find new approaches that bring out their better side.

When people at work engage in unpleasant behavior, our reactions are often to avoid them, complain, or write them off. While these responses may provide a momentary sense of satisfaction, none of them improve the relationship. In contrast, when we make an effort to "walk in the other person's shoes," we can begin to gain some insight into the reasons for his or her behavior. We may never end up liking or approving of the difficult person, but when we start to appreciate what makes him or her "tick," we enhance our ability to work with the person effectively.

This program provides strategies for moving from impasse to insight with difficult people on the job. It will be especially useful to you if you are willing to take responsibility for your own growth and development . . . regardless of your job or role in the organization.

You will have the opportunity:

- To examine a difficult work relationship

- To learn ways to "get curious," rather than furious

- To plan a new approach to a difficult person

- To select "experiments in change" at work

We all know people we find difficult or challenging to work with. Do any of these "Challengers" sound familiar to you?

Customers

Carol Complainer: *"Is this the best you can do?"*
Harvey Hierarchy: *"What's the name of your supervisor?"*

Co-Workers

Needy Nan: *"Can you help me out? Want to hear about my weekend?"*
Superior Stan: *"Mistakes? I never make any. Unlike you!"*

Direct Reports

Late Nate: *"No, it was yesterday that the bus was late. Today I had to take my son to the dentist."*
Pathetic Patty: *"I can't do this! You'll have to show me how."*

The Boss

Ted Tyrant: *"I'd rather be feared than loved!"*
Carla Cryptic: *"I don't have time to go over this. Just figure it out yourself."*

How would you rate your ability to bring out the best in someone you find difficult?

4 = consistently   3 = often   2 = sometimes   1 = never

___ 1. I listen attentively to the person, without "running my own tape."

___ 2. I ask questions that draw out the person's thoughts and feelings.

___ 3. I consult others who may have insights about the person.

___ 4. I "walk in the other person's shoes" to appreciate how he or she looks at a situation.

___ 5. I look below the surface to understand what the other person may be anxious about.

For each relationship, list some of the people who belong in that category for you. Put an asterisk (*) beside the names of those whom you find challenging or difficult to work with.

My Customers _____

_____

_____

_____

My Co-Workers _____

_____

_____

_____

My Direct Reports _____

_____

_____

_____

My Boss _____

_____

_____

_____

If we want to bring out the better side of a Challenger, we need to get curious, rather than furious, when we are faced with his or her difficult behavior. We don't have to like the person or approve of his or her behavior. But if we can get curious about *why* the person acts as he or she does, rather than get upset about *what* he or she does, we may gain perspective and find more productive ways to approach the person. Here are five ways to get curious:

1. *Take time to listen*—give the person your full attention and don't interrupt. Paraphrase what you hear to let the person know you've heard and understood.

2. *Ask questions*—use probing, open-ended questions to draw out the person's thoughts and feelings, such as:

    What were your reactions/thoughts about. . . ?

    Can you give me an example or two?

    How come?

    Why do you feel that way?

    What makes that important for you?

3. *Consult others*—seek out someone who seems to have more success with your Challenger and ask for his or her perspective and for suggestions about new approaches to try.

4. *Walk in the person's shoes*—try looking at events from your Challenger's point of view. Ask yourself how the other person might regard situations differently than you do.

5. *Relate in new ways*—identify the way you typically approach the person and experiment with a dramatically different behavior. Notice what happens.

Which of the following behaviors might be a good approach to take with your Challenger?

❑ Take extra time to build rapport and establish trust.

❑ Be firmer and more consistent about what you expect.

❑ Take a positive approach by reinforcing and encouraging the person.

❑ Ask the person to tell you about his or her views, needs, and concerns.

❑ Back off on a big change; focus on little ones.

❑ Be more honest and straightforward about what you think and feel.

❑ Be more persistent with your efforts to influence the person.

All human beings have three basic needs. Which might your Challenger be particularly anxious about?

❑ **Control**—having power over our lives, being in the driver's seat

❑ **Connection**—belonging, being supported, loved, accepted

❑ **Competence**—being successful, demonstrating mastery and being recognized for it

Based on your selection, which of the following behaviors might be good approaches to try with your Challenger?

If your Challenger is anxious about *control*, you might . . .

❑ Keep him or her informed and up-to-date

❑ Offer choices and decisions

❑ Seek agreement (*"I thought I'd do X. Is that okay with you?"*)

❑ Ask: *"What role would you like to have in this project?"*

If your Challenger is anxious about *connection*, you might . . .

❑ Make a point of showing him or her attention—when it's convenient for you

❑ Tactfully and directly set limits when he or she wants too much of your time

❑ Offer greetings or conversation in low-keyed, small doses

❑ Ask a question you know he or she can answer "yes" to

If your Challenger is anxious about *competence*, you might . . .

❑ Give genuine positive feedback when you can

❑ Avoid putting him or her on the spot in front of others

❑ Give a task you know he or she can do successfully

❑ Praise accomplishments matter-of-factly, not effusively

TRY IT: EXPERIMENTS IN CHANGE

Select one of the following "experiments in change" to do within the next week.

❑ *Improving Listening*

Think of the person you consider the best listener you know, someone you invariably feel comfortable talking with. For a week, study his or her nonverbal behavior during conversations the person has with you or others. What does the person do that conveys interest and acceptance? Write down some of the behaviors you notice the person using. Next, notice whether any of these behaviors are part of your own present repertoire. If not, which of the behaviors would you be willing to try? Choose one or two and practice them.

❑ *Recognizing Anxieties*

Think of someone you simply do not understand at all. Think about this person's behavior in a few key situations. What does he or she seem most anxious about: control, connection, or competence? Is this different from your own usual concerns? When you recognize his or her source of anxiety, do you understand the person better? Will you change any of your own behavior in dealing with this person in the future?

❑ *Understanding Differences*

Identify someone at work who's as different from you as possible. On a 1 to 10 scale, where 1 is the lowest and 10 the highest rating, rate how well you understand this person's values, assumptions, and motivation. Now list some of the ways this person is different from you, including goals, personal style, and demographic factors. Which of these differences may be interfering with your ability to understand and relate to this person? Try to imagine yourself as him or her, seeing the world through his or her eyes. How do you feel? How do things seem different to you? Now re-rate your understanding of the person. Is there a change?

❑ *Asking Questions*

Identify someone at work you find difficult to understand or relate to. Now think of a particular issue that involves both of you, such as a project you are working on together, a person or client whom you both deal with, or a policy that affects you both. Imagine you are going to interview the person you identified about the matter you selected. Write a list of open-ended questions you could use to uncover the person's thoughts and feelings about the subject. See how probing you can make your questions. When you are satisfied with your list of questions, imagine you are the other person and answer them. If you want to learn whether your answers are on target, there's one sure way to find out: go ahead and pose your questions to the person!

How to Bring Out the Better Side of Difficult People: Participant's Workbook

What stands out for you as the key points from today's session?

_____

_____

_____

_____

_____

_____

_____

_____

_____

_____

_____

_____

_____

BRINGING OUT THE BETTER SIDE
OF DIFFICULT PEOPLE

Reading

When people at work engage in unpleasant behavior, it's only human to be annoyed or even furious. Typically, we might cope by doing any or all of the following:

- Avoiding them whenever possible

- Complaining about them to a trusted colleague

- Writing them off as people who can't or won't change their ways

As much as any of these challenging people at work frustrate us, the "people smart" thing to do is get curious *why* they act the way they do rather than merely get upset about *what* they do. This involves trying to develop an "empathic understanding" of a person who is puzzling. What is it like to be in this person's "shoes"?

You may not like or approve of the other person's behavior. Certainly, no one should tolerate irresponsible behavior. Nonetheless, it pays to explore why the person acts in the ways he or she does because:

- It may unlock new ways to relate to the person that will be productive for both of you.

- It may give you a new perspective on the person and help you gain some distance and avoid taking what the person does too personally.

- It may also win the appreciation of that person and serve as a basis for a better relationship.

In contrast, failing to explore possible causes of the person's behavior not only perpetuates the impasse, but also leads to increasing frustration and, ultimately, cynicism. When we accumulate too many "hopeless cases" we may become even quicker to write people off and find ourselves walled off from others. Let's look at an example of how "furious" might begin shifting to "curious":

> *In the accounting office where I work as office manager, there is an accountant named Helen, who couldn't be more different from me. She always seems down in the dumps, grumbling under her breath and looking angry. She doesn't respond to jokes and never joins the rest of us in the lunchroom. She just focuses on her work and keeps reminding everybody how much responsibility she has.*

I'm a much more social person. I always get my work done, but I also like to talk with people throughout the day, pass along humorous stories via email, and so forth. If we were two of the seven dwarfs, I'd be Happy and Helen would be Grumpy. I know we also have significant differences in our personal lives. Helen is a single mother, living with her elderly parents—both of whom have had some serious health problems—in their home. I am married and live with my husband and two of my three young adult daughters in our own home.

Have I written off Helen? I guess if I were in her shoes, I'd feel overwhelmed with responsibilities. Raising a child alone, caring for elderly parents, and then coming to a job where she's trying to help fatten other people's bankrolls, while she doesn't even own a home . . . that's pretty bleak. If I were in a survival mode like Helen's, some of the stuff I talk about, and certainly many of the email jokes I circulate, would probably look pretty superficial.

What really prompted me to reconsider my attitude toward Helen was an office crisis. Someone made a mistake and overlooked an important deadline with one of the accounts. It was Helen who caught the error in time to request an extension. I still wouldn't want to live with my nose to the grindstone the way she does, but maybe she has a point about responsibility. It rocks my boat to think that perhaps I've been a bit smug in my attitude toward her.

Although she hasn't become Helen's buddy, the office manager has taken a crucial step forward in their relationship. By walking in Helen's shoes for a few paces and accepting the possibility that Helen's differences aren't necessarily all deficits, she has opened the door just enough to gain a small glimpse of who may be on the other side.

Five Tips to Understand Other People Better

Whenever we become frustrated by another person at work, that frustration can eat away our energy to perform at our best. The good news is that we have several opportunities to "become curious rather than furious."

1. Take Time to Listen to This Person. When this challenging person talks, give him or her your full attention, without "running your own tape" about what you'll say next. Try to avoid interrupting what he or she is saying or simply tuning the person out. You might even paraphrase what you hear the person saying, so that he or she gets the idea that you're really listening.

Undoubtedly, you've heard much of what the person is about to tell you before. People have a tendency to repeat themselves. We all have "stump speeches," much like politicians. However, if you encourage the person to keep talking, he or she might go beyond the usual stump speech and tell you things he or she has never said before. That's when you begin to get the information to help you really understand where this person is coming from. You must make a clear decision that the other person is someone worth listening to and give him or her your full concentration. Imagine a spotlight shining on the speaker. If you are doing something else that could distract you, stop. Instead of working at your desk, for example, consider standing up and moving to another location, in or outside your office, to help you focus on the speaker. Instruct others to not interrupt your time with this person, if necessary.

2. Ask This Person Questions About His or Her Thoughts and Feelings. Use open-ended questions to draw out new information and clarify what you are hearing. This is especially important when trying to understand a relatively taciturn individual who keeps a lot inside. Open-ended questions invite the speaker to expand or elaborate on her message. They offer more leeway to respond and share. *"What was the upsetting part for you about what he said?" "How do you foresee things getting better on this project?" "Why do you think Bob was so quiet at the meeting?"* Use open-ended questions to encourage others to "open up" and share thoughts, feelings, and opinions. By doing so, you increase your chances of learning what's really important to them. Moreover, the person may respond favorably to your attention and interest.

There are many ways to do this, such as stating or asking:

- *"I'm not sure I know what your thoughts are about. . . ."*

- *"Tell me more about this."*

- *"What were your reactions/thoughts about. . . ?"*

- *"Can you give me an example or two?"*

- *"How come? Why do you feel that way?"*

- *"I've never asked you about. . . ."*

3. Consult Other People Who May Have Insights About This Person. Who seems to have more success with this person? Ask for his or her perspective on your Challenger and for suggestions on new approaches to try. Even if you find that everyone you know has the same feelings about this person as you do, they may have different ways of coping. You might approach a colleague and say: *"I've been really frustrated by [name of person]. What works for you in dealing with [him or her]?"* The person you are consulting may have some knowledge you lack or a terrific suggestion about how to deal with this challenging individual. If none is forthcoming, at least there are now two of you trying to put your heads together about this person rather than tackling the situation all by yourself.

4. Try "Walking in His or Her Shoes" by Looking at Events from This Person's Point of View. Imagine you *are* the other person and ask yourself how a specific situation would look to you, what you'd be feeling, and what your concerns might be. This is not an easy task. It's hard to put aside how you would look at the situation.

One suggestion that might help is to appreciate that the other person may look at things differently than you do. For example, you might see the assignments you receive as an opportunity to show others how capable you are. The other person might view assignments as simply a job to be done. Although each of us has our own preferences and style, it's important to recognize that *different* doesn't necessarily mean *better* (or worse). Are right-handed people "better" than lefties?

Here are some ways in which the other person may be different from you:

spontaneous	careful
social	private
emotional	analytic
take charge	responsive
competitive	collaborative
give opinions	ask questions
intense	easygoing
focused	multi-tasking
confronting	avoiding
self-oriented	group-oriented
respect for talent	respect for authority
loose	rule-oriented

Reflecting on how the other person may have a contrasting style to your own will help you appreciate his or her "shoes." Notice, for example, that the other end of the continuum from "spontaneous" is "careful," not "rigid." Like Helen, the accountant, someone who is less freewheeling and more deliberate than you may have a unique contribution to make.

5. Try Out Some New Ways to Relate to the Person. Identify how you typically "dance" with that person. Are you avoiding? Critical? Forgiving? Demanding? Be curious enough to see what would happen if you acted dramatically different. For example, you might consider one of the following new behaviors:

- Take extra time to build rapport and establish trust with this person.

- Be firmer and more consistent about what you expect from this person.

- Take a positive approach by reinforcing and encouraging this person.

- Ask this person to tell you about his or her views, needs, and concerns.

- Back off on a big change; focus on little ones.

- Be more honest and straightforward with this person about what you think and feel.

- Be more persistent with your efforts to influence this person. Don't let up.

Looking at Challenging People as Anxious People

We realize that finding the energy to act on these five ways to understand others better can often be a tall order. You may be so frustrated, angry, or pessimistic at this point in the relationship that it would take an awful lot of resolve to refocus.

One of the best ways to develop anew the energy to be "curious rather than furious" is to consider that all human beings, the challenging as well as the pleasant, have three basic human needs:

- *Control* is our need to have power over our life, being in the driver's seat instead of the passenger seat.

- *Connection* is our need for belonging, support, love, and acceptance.

- *Competence* is our need for success, demonstrating mastery and being recognized for doing so.

At any given time, we may be anxious about obtaining one or more of these needs. To lessen the anxiety, we might go to one of two extremes . . . overly pursue the fulfillment of the need or avoid situations in which the need arises. For example, someone who is anxious about *control* might act like a "control freak," someone who needs everything done his or her way. In contrast, someone else who is anxious about *control* may decide to let others call the shots. Someone anxious about *connection* might act like a social leech, while someone else might withdraw or reject others. Someone anxious about *competence* might be a braggart, while someone else might act like a failure.

Imagine you had a co-worker named Steve. Here is what he's like, if you only look at him with fury rather than curiosity:

> *Steve is arrogant, opinionated, and sloppy about his work . . . yet highly critical of others. He often makes crude or insensitive comments to people and reacts very defensively to any type of suggestion or criticism, no matter how constructive.*
>
> *Steve "stumbled" onto his job at our company. Despite the training he's received, the job is a little out of his league. He knows it. And he knows that everyone else knows it. Yet he gives off an air of superiority. He won't ask for help or advice. And if help or advice is offered, he rejects it.*

How might you apply the 3 C's (*Control, Connection, and Competence*) to Steve to better understand his behavior?

Perhaps Steve may be using his arrogance to push people away and avoid connection because he's afraid others will reject him. (And is it just possible that the culture at this company is not as accepting as it could be?) Or Steve may be very insecure about his competence and thinks that he's safer if he keeps people at a distance (and when a mistake leads people to conclude you're "out of your league," can you blame him?). If we can understand Steve's anxieties, we may be able to relate to him better. For instance, maybe it would be better to connect with him, especially when he's not being obnoxious, and perhaps he'll feel more accepted and less likely to push people away. Maybe if his co-workers complimented his occasional successes, he might be more open to their criticism.

When you think about the people whom you find challenging, consider what may be making them anxious and use that insight to look at them differently and perhaps act toward them differently.

When someone is anxious about *control,* you might . . .

- Keep him or her informed and up-to-date

- Offer choices and decisions

- Invite "rubber stamp" choices (*"I thought I'd do X. Is that okay with you?"*)

- Ask: *"What role would you like to have in this project?"*

When someone is anxious about *connection,* you might . . .

- Make a point of showing the person attention when it's convenient for you

- Tactfully and directly set limits when he or she wants too much of your time

- Offer greetings or conversation in low-keyed, small doses

- Ask a question you know he or she can answer "yes" to

When someone is anxious about *competence,* you might . . .

- Give genuine positive feedback when you can

- Avoid putting the person on the spot in front of others

- Give her or him a task you know she or he can do successfully

- Praise accomplishments matter-of-factly, rather than effusively

We can't give "makeovers" that will turn difficult people into delights. But if we put our energy into understanding our Challengers, we may be able to present them with our better side—and tap into theirs as well.

Three Challenging Situations

Below are three situations that may have occurred in your own work. Read the question posed in each situation and see what an effective solution looks like.

Situation 1
"My new boss acts like he knows more than I do about producing our product, even though this is his first year with the company. He doesn't show respect for my knowledge and competence. How am I going to work with him?"

When we don't like or don't understand someone, we often have a tendency to write off that person and declare him or her a lost cause. Dismissing or labeling the person may give us a momentary sense of satisfaction, but it doesn't shed any light on the person's behavior. The "people smart" alternative is to make a serious effort to understand the person's motives and perspective. This is not the same as liking or accepting the person; it's more like approaching him or her scientifically.

Once you've made the crucial decision to try to understand your boss, there are numerous ways to go about it. One is to ask him questions. We don't mean give him the third degree, but rather, interview him in a friendly way to learn more about his views and experiences. You might ask him how he's doing at getting used to the place, what he studied in college, where he's from, et cetera. Listen attentively and responsively. You can also give some thought to how differences between you may be hindering understanding. Differences in style, age, gender, and culture, for example, can sometimes lead to misunderstanding and conflicting viewpoints. If your boss is a young guy who grew up in an age of instant technology (while you didn't), perhaps you have different expectations about how long it takes to learn something new.

You can also try to look below the surface and ask yourself what your boss might be anxious about. We all need the 3 C's: control, connection with others, and competence. But sometimes people are overly anxious about one or more of these issues. As the "new kid on the block," your boss may be anxious about whether people more senior than he see him as a competent, capable manager. People who are anxious about competence are very sensitive about appearing uninformed or out of their league in any way. Asking your advice may simply be too threatening for your boss to do right now. If you try to help put him at ease and acknowledge his strengths, he may become more open to you in time.

Situation 2

"I have a colleague who's a total piece of work. She's a real perfectionist. It takes her forever to get anything done, which makes for big headaches when we have to work on a project together. And of course she's never satisfied with what anyone else produces. She doesn't mesh with the team. For instance, on casual Friday, when everyone wears jeans to work, she comes in wearing one of her prissy little suits. She seems to keep people at a distance. I'm generally a pretty friendly, easygoing person, but she's just too much of a challenge to get along with. Do I really have to make the effort, or can I just try to work around her?"

It isn't very difficult to work with people we enjoy and identify with. Working "people smart" entails finding ways to understand and reach out to those we'd rather avoid. You never have to like this person or give her your vote as employee of the month. But if you find a way to work with her you'll probably spend less time feeling aggravated and *you* will look like a real team player.

Consider your co-worker's needs. She seems pretty anxious about control, as if she only feels comfortable when she's the one carrying the ball. What happens when you try to pull the ball away from someone like that? She just holds on more tightly. If you *accept* that she has this anxiety (even though you don't share it), it becomes easier to choose an approach that may better meet her needs.

How to Bring Out the Better Side of Difficult People: Participant's Workbook

When you work with her on a project, make a point of seeking her input up-front about how the end product should look, how much time the project will require, et cetera. Keep her informed about your own progress (not because you need a watchdog, but because her anxiety requires it).

By your description, she is out of sync with the style of the group. Maybe she's anxious about being included and anticipates rejection. It's not your job to become her therapist, but if you are persistent about reaching out in a low-keyed way (just saying good morning or asking how her weekend went), over time she may become a little less distant with you. Eventually, others in the office will be seeking out your advice on how to deal with her.

Situation 3

"One of my direct reports seems to be on the skids. He's normally a good worker, but lately his reports are just not up to par. When I tried to discuss it with him and offer some suggestions for improvement, he became really defensive. I feel like I'm in a bind. I don't see how I can just ignore what's going on, but I don't want to pry or be inappropriately personal either. What's the best way to help this guy?"

A doctor wouldn't treat symptoms without making a diagnosis. A good mechanic wouldn't try to fix your car without figuring out what's broken. Before you can resolve whatever problem is going on with your direct report, you need to understand it. We suggest you "interview" rather than interrogate him with the goal of learning how *he* sees the situation.

Interviewing is a form of active listening aimed at uncovering information—without putting the other person on the spot. When you interview, some key behaviors include:

- Ask questions and dig for deeper understanding.

- Solicit the other person's viewpoint, while holding back on your own.

- Seek clarification and illuminate how the other person is feeling.

- Demonstrate understanding of what the person is sharing.

Make some time to sit down with your direct report and start by stating in a calm, straightforward way that you've noticed his recent reports aren't up to his usual high standards and you'd like to understand how he sees the situation. You might ask: *"How do you think this report compares with what you usually turn in?"* Once you get the ball rolling, make a point of being receptive and responsive to anything he says. An excellent way to do this is by paraphrasing.

When you paraphrase, you feed back, succinctly and in your own words, the most important elements of the person's message. Paraphrasing gets a bad name because people often do it poorly, either by parroting the same words the person just said or by using some hackneyed formula, like *"So I hear you saying. . . ."* In contrast, when you capture and reflect the heart of what someone tells you, you begin to gain the person's trust and encourage him or her to open up further. So the interview with your direct report might sound something like this:

You: *"How do you think this report compares with what you usually turn in?"*

D.R.: *"All right, well, it's a little below par. I'm sorry."*

You: *"So you're not entirely happy with it either. Can you tell me what you think may have contributed to the change?"*

D.R.: *"Well, since Jim was transferred to sales, I'm not getting the same information I used to get. I guess the report suffers for it."*

You: *"You sound frustrated."*

D.R.: *"I am! I don't like doing a second-rate job, but I don't see how I can produce the same quality in the same time with less support."*

You can move to a problem-solving mode after you have adequately explored the situation. Your solutions are more likely to be effective when you understand the problem.

Notes

Notes